My Journ

The story of one woman's path into
ordained priesthood in the
Catholic Church

Caryl Conroy Johnson

May you always enjoy the great gift of inner freedom.

Caryl Conroy Johnson

Copyright © 2016 by Caryl Conroy Johnson

All rights reserved. No part of this publication may be reproduced or transmitted in any form without prior permission in writing from the publisher.

Questions regarding permissions should be sent to ccjohnson2236@aol.com.

Front Cover Photo:
Summit of Table Mountain, Cape Town, South Africa

Top Back Cover Photo:
Table Mountain, Cape Town, South Africa

Background Back Cover Photo:
Jonkershoek Nature Reserve, Stellenbosch, South Africa

ISBN 978-1-5323-1083-6

My Journey Into Freedom

I dedicate this story to all who long to be free to be who they are…

A special dedication of gratitude to all who have journeyed in faith with me, especially

- my husband, Stan—my lifelong hiking partner on the journey of my life—for his faithful and loving companionship and for always encouraging me to follow my heart

- our children, Dayna, Tahra, and Shaen, for their adventurous, supportive, and free spirits and all they have birthed in me

- my parents, Dot and Bill Conroy, for creating me, planting the seeds of a strong and questioning faith, and embodying God to me from the beginning, and to my stepmother, Rose Kelly Conroy, who was a wisdom-woman to me as I made my choices for freedom

Introduction

The story of my faith journey is deeply personal and yet communal. It is the story of my call, as a woman, to priesthood in the Catholic church—at its heart a journey into freedom. Although there have been moments of great pain, the joys have far outweighed the suffering. In the Ignatian[1] spirit, I consider all as gift. You will notice photographs throughout the text; these are trails I have happily hiked in the United States and other countries. These places are special to me because I feel a spiritual connection whenever I am in nature; God and I bond on these trails, and the paths reflect how we adventurously hike through life together.

As I relate my story, I do so with gratitude for all that has been and hopeful expectation for all that will be.

This is the back of Caryl's favorite hiking tee shirt.

Three Conversations and a Question

How in the world did I become a Catholic priest? Did I ever have an inkling this would happen?

As I look back on my journey, I remember three foretelling conversations that made me think there was something more ahead. I just didn't know what that "something" was.

God knocked on my door several times through a special woman in my life. Her name is Mary LeFever. Mary was my Brownie leader when I was 8 years old; she watched me "grow up." I have always admired Mary, particularly her openness to new ways of thinking and being. She is a faith-filled woman who founded a Montessori school in the late 1960s and who is active in community events. When I was on the pastoral staff at St. Francis of Assisi Parish, Mary was part of the bereavement team. We also are members of the same faith-sharing group. All this background is to say that for many years Mary and I have traveled various roads together. On our shared journey she often said to me, "Caryl, you should be a priest." Other times she would say, "I hope I live long enough to see you ordained a priest." I would laugh because the rules didn't allow women to be ordained. How could I take her comments seriously? But I did hear them, felt them deeply, and knew she was serious in conveying them. Later on in my journey when I was leaving the St. Francis staff and discerning the next step, I finally realized that, in various ways and through various friends, I needed to start listening more fully and with a deeper understanding, that maybe God was trying to tell me something. I asked Mary what she saw in me that made her think I should be a priest... I have no doubt that Mary embodied God's voice as I felt God calling me to "something" more...

On another occasion, during a pastoral visit I helped my friend and her family plan their mom's funeral Mass. To close our time together, I led us in prayer. Afterwards, she looked at me and said, "How about if you say the funeral Mass?!" In that moment I felt God calling me to "something" more...

During the 8 years I attended charismatic prayer group meetings, I frequently shared reflections on the scriptures. I also regularly shared my experiences in nature and the beautiful outdoors, connecting them with a spiritual message. God spoke to me through nature, and I was grateful to be able to share these revelations. On several occasions the prayer group leaders told me that I had a special and unusual gift. They weren't quite sure how to name it and were discerning what that gift was. They called it "a word of knowledge." I felt God calling me to "something" more...

Here is my story.

The Gift of Freedom

Inner freedom is at the heart of my story. I came to see I needed to be free in order to fully serve God and God's people. To follow God's Spirit rather than rely on dogma and law, I needed to be liberated. To be who I really am, I had to be free. It was a journey of struggle, joy, suffering, and pain that brought me to a deep, liberating place within myself. Inner freedom was essential for me to walk the path of my call into priestly ordination. It is a gift for which I am deeply grateful and one I draw from daily as I continue to answer God's call.

The Beginnings

I was born in 1954 into a traditional family of Irish-Italian heritage in America where faith in God was a core value. We were a family of four—my mom, dad, older brother, Bill, and me—and we enjoyed a comfortable but far from wealthy lifestyle. Our loving God played an important daily role in my childhood. I learned that God was my friend and was with me in life's everyday moments. My family prayed each day before meals and at bedtime. We worshipped at St. Francis of Assisi Catholic Church (located in Springfield, Delaware County, Pennsylvania, in the Philadelphia Archdiocese) every Sunday. My parents in their loving, supportive marriage were my primary teachers of faith. They reflected a healthy image of God to me through their unconditional love, sense of fairness, forgiveness, and zest for life. They also taught me the importance of healthy, constructive questioning and did not blindly accept every church dogma and teaching. Through their example I was permitted to wonder and question and still remain part of a community without agreeing with everything. Through their modeling I learned how to make decisions of conscience through prayerful discernment. My parents responded to church laws in thoughtful, reflective ways and were not constrained by laws they believed were unjust and not in keeping with God's ways. For example, at that time Catholics were not supposed to go to a non-Catholic church. Not only did my parents go to non-

Catholic churches—usually for weddings and funerals—they also participated in the service. They also questioned the way the church treated those who were divorced. Their open-mindedness created a safe environment for me to question, disagree, and make decisions of conscience that were not in keeping with church law. This was a critical foundation for my future. An early example of this occurred when I was about 10 years old. When our school classes attended Mass, the boys sat on one side and the girls on the other. When Mass was over, the boys were always dismissed first. One day I asked my mom, "Why do the boys always get to leave first?" She said, "Because Jesus was a boy." Well, that did not sit well at all with me! I told her the fair way would be to take turns. Even at that young age, I noticed and questioned what I saw as unequal treatment. A second illustration occurred when I was about 13 years old. I had a conversation with my dad that has remained with me. It was the late 1960s, and the Vatican II liturgy changes were being implemented. My dad went along with the changes but said, "That will be it for the changes—no more will happen." I immediately shot back, "Oh no, if we don't keep changing, we'll have the same problems as before Vatican II." Something inside me knew that change was important to growth, relevancy, and a more meaningful way of experiencing and worshipping God. My dad, just as my mom in the previous example, only listened and did not challenge me.

  My education at the Catholic elementary and high school reinforced their teaching. My elementary education at St. Francis of Assisi School offered me a solid faith foundation. I went on to Cardinal O'Hara High School in

Springfield, an archdiocesan high school with 4,000 students. The religion courses challenged me to think critically about moral choices. During these classes we considered all aspects of faith and moral issues. This taught me that a well-formed decision of conscience consisted of weighing alternatives and a decision based on core beliefs. The teachers encouraged us to articulate our doubts and questions, which often challenged the status quo. I am deeply grateful to my teachers and fellow students for the open, edgy discussions and challenges of faith that emerged from these classes. Some friends who attended other schools did not experience that kind of openness, so I am particularly thankful for this education. I also experienced personal growth in the philosophy and theology courses that were part of my undergraduate business degree at St. Joseph's University in Philadelphia. This provided the foundation and backdrop for the significant journey that lay ahead.

Routeburn Track, Queenstown, New Zealand

As an Adult

As I moved further into my early adult years, my faith continued to deepen. In 1976, I married my lifelong partner, Stan. Stan and I were of different Christian traditions. He was a practicing Presbyterian but had Quaker, Baptist, and even some Christian Science roots in his background. During our dating relationship and into our marriage, we engaged in deep discussions of our personal beliefs. Although I had certain issues with the dogma of the church, at this point they were fragments in my mind and were not stumbling blocks to my faith development. Our many commonalities and profound respect for our differences provided a strong relational foundation from which we grew. It propelled us to talk in depth about our faith in God and the importance of giving our children a firm faith foundation. Stan and I chose to raise our children Catholic and expose them to other faith traditions. They attended the local public schools and were friends with students of many different faiths. They also attended our parish religious education program and later were actively involved in the relational youth ministry program in our parish.

I believe our children benefited from seeing how we honestly and respectfully handled our differences. It gave them, as well as us, a broader perspective and richer tradition to draw from.

Crowder Mountain State Park, North Carolina

Twists and Turns

Throughout my twenties, I experienced a growing dissatisfaction with many church rules, regulations, and teachings. These were related to a number of issues and led to a critical point in my spiritual journey. In 1983, at the age of 29, I experienced the first of my deep inner struggles and came within an eyelash of leaving the Catholic church. I became angry with the church and deeply hurt by her position on the role of women in the church and other issues. I was distressed by the church's exclusion of women from ordained priesthood and other ministerial roles. Being ineligible for priesthood purely because I was born a woman struck at the heart of my being. The pain of this discrimination was undeniable. This was a deep-seated pain that had gnawed at my heart and mind for many years. Although I had one foot out the door and was hanging on by a thread, I continued to worship every Sunday. My faith in God was solid, but my commitment to living out that faith in the Catholic church was on very shaky ground. I knew, however, that leaving the church I loved dearly would not be a quick decision. As deep and heart-wrenching as the pain was, my love for the church ran just as deep. I took time to work through the pain and see where God was leading me. I prayed with it, thought about it, and struggled mightily until I came to clarity. Although I had discerned important issues prior to this one, this is the first time I consciously used the word discernment to describe my decision-making process. Logic told me to leave, yet my heart told me to stay. Why I experienced this struggle at this particular time remains a mystery. What I do know is that it was a critical step along the path of my deepening journey into God.

    I began to emerge from this 10-month inner struggle during Christian Unity Week in 1984, when I experienced a conversion of heart. I was drawn back to the church and began to develop a deeper, more personal, two-way relationship with Jesus. A deeply spiritual lay woman was instrumental in this experience. As I received bread from her during a Christian Unity Week ritual, I felt a sensation course through my entire being. In this moment God touched me deeply through her. Following this weeklong celebration, I experienced an insatiable thirst for scripture. It caught me off-guard because prior to this I had seldom read scripture. During my formative years, the Catholic church did not encourage the laity to read and pray with the scriptures. This unquenchable desire to read and pray the scriptures was a graced surprise—the Spirit of God took over and I could not get enough of it!

In addition to reading the bible, I began to pray contemplatively each day and meet regularly with a spiritual director. My initial spiritual director was a parish priest who companioned me through this time of searching and growth. He helped me come to a deeper understanding of my relationship with God. I will always be grateful for his spiritual guidance. I also prayed weekly with a charismatic prayer group, which deepened my love of scripture. This Spirit-led forum also gave me the opportunity to share my reflections on God's Word.

Early on with this prayer group, I attended a Life in the Spirit Seminar, which was transformational. During the seminar attendees are "baptized in the Spirit." During this baptism the prayer group leaders lay hands on and pray over each candidate. I felt a spiritual excitement build within me as the moment approached. As the leaders laid hands on me and prayed, I felt a strong, burning sensation in my arm, hot like the Pentecost "tongues of fire." This was a life-changing moment for me. I believed in my heart that something was happening at another level. The Spirit of God was opening me to a new path and a deeper experience of the divine.

All of these experiences laid the groundwork for a journey with God that—to this day—continues to surprise, excite, stimulate, and free me. So I laced up my hiking boots, gathered my support network, and started walking! In my parish I continued to be involved in several ministries on a volunteer basis. While we were raising young children, I chose to stop working full-time. During these years I needed adult companionship and intellectual stimulation and chose to serve in parish ministry and further my education. Having earned a B. S. in management and worked as an analyst in international market research, an MBA was a logical next step. While taking my MBA, however, I began to feel a hunger deep within me to study theology. So I transitioned from business studies and enrolled in the Church Ministry Training Program at St. Charles Seminary in Philadelphia. Upon completion, if women had been eligible to be deacons, I most likely would have begun the permanent diaconate program. Because this avenue was closed, I enrolled in the M. A. in Religious Studies Program at St. Charles and graduated in 1992.

Graduation from St. Charles Seminary 1992

Family Photo—Graduation from St. Charles Seminary 1992

Tyler Arboretum, Media, Pennsylvania

Forgiveness and Freedom

About this time I had a second major crisis of faith—again related to the role of women in the church. This turned out to be a critical point in my journey into freedom. About a decade earlier, in 1984, I had come to the deep realization that I would always remain in the Catholic church. So here I was again, up against that familiar stone wall: How could the faith that I loved prevent women from being ordained? I didn't know how I would reconcile these two deep-seated realities. The pain was fierce, and the uncertainty was frightening. To work through this monumental struggle, I did a lot of theological reading on both sides of the ordination issue. After reading these position papers and carefully discerning their content, I believed even more strongly that both women and men should be eligible for ordination. In addition to these writings, I read *A Concise History of the Catholic Church* by Thomas Bokenkotter. This opened me to the many opinions put forth not only in the Christian communities of the early centuries, but also during the sessions of Vatican II in the 1960s. It gave me more understanding of the give and take of diverse opinions in the church. I came to realize that many voices expressing different viewpoints have always been expressed in the church. I came to see that I, too, could stay in the church and have a different opinion.

Although this realization was now clear, I still needed to address the hurt and pain that continued to eat away my insides. I knew I had to forgive the church. Although no priest had ever told me that he was sorry for my pain or the injustice of excluding women from ordination, I realized I did not need his apology in order to forgive the church. Theological and historical readings, related discussions with my spiritual director, and a personal choice to forgive helped me move to a place of inner peace with the ordination issue. I was in a love relationship with the church and knew the only way I could continue in this relationship was to forgive. So I did. This was a very significant moment for me. I had struggled for many years with the church's dogmatic intransigence on the ordination of women and had worked through this issue that pained me deeply. Yet there was a missing piece that needed healing. I wanted to be free from the strident feelings of anger, frustration, and discrimination that welled up within me when I tried to discuss this issue. Through honest self-confrontation I found the missing piece was forgiveness. During Lent of 1993, with over 200 people in attendance, I gave a personal witness on forgiveness at our parish mission. I publicly forgave the church for the pain she caused me and asked the church to forgive me for thinking my opinion was the only right one. In this moment I felt completely exposed and vulnerable. I shared my story publicly in the hope that it would help someone who had also felt deeply hurt by the church.

After the service, I felt touched by many people who told me how moved they were by my witness. One woman described it as something everyone could relate to, thought-provoking, an experience she would go home and ponder for awhile. Several years later when I was assisting at a funeral, a family member spoke to me about my witness. She had been at the mission and with great emotion shared how deeply my words had affected her. It was clear God had touched her at the core through my words spoken years earlier.

      On emotional, intellectual, and spiritual levels something inside me had shifted, and I took the first step toward freedom from the deep pain and strident attitude that nagged my soul. I had given a three-minute witness on my personal experience of forgiveness, and those three minutes altered my life forever. I was never the same. To this day the mention of the word forgiveness evokes strong feelings within me. Theological readings, many conversations, and contemplative prayer were all important parts of my discernment that led to healing. But it was forgiveness, honestly facing what bound me up, that freed me. Jesus touched my heart in that moment, and because Jesus freed me, I am now able to lovingly and freely speak of my experience. This deeper healing was unexpected, yet one that continues to touch me profoundly. I have been freed at a deeper level. Freed to tell my story and speak out clearly to more people. Freed to be who I am—to be radical, inclusive, transforming love to God's people. I continue to give thanks to God for God's extraordinary gift of freeing forgiveness. My relationship with God was reset, now based on freedom, forgiveness, and love.

Ayers Rock, Outback, Australia

A New Journey

When I completed my education at St. Charles Seminary in 1992, the next step in my journey began to unfold. After an 18-month process discerning between pastoral and educational ministries, it became clear that pastoral ministry was my vocation. I then actively went in search of these positions and applied with the archdiocesan office. Before I interviewed with them, the pastor at St. Francis of Assisi Parish, Springfield, hired me as a Pastoral Associate. In 1994 I began this new journey. My pastor showed courage in hiring me, a married woman, onto the staff. This was a new position, and he gave me the freedom to walk into this role, shape its path, and use my pastoral gifts in serving God's people. I am truly grateful to him to this day for that opportunity to serve and to journey more deeply into God's call. As a member of the pastoral staff I was involved primarily in bereavement ministry, ministry to the sick, high school youth ministry, worship, and interfaith events. The work was life-giving. I loved the people I ministered to and worked with, and I felt my soul singing.

We continued to raise our family, and my ministry work was not only enriching for me personally but also for them. Then in 2003, I faced a third major crisis of faith related to the role of women in the church, an experience that resulted in a life-changing moment during a weeklong, silent retreat. As part of this retreat, I met daily with a spiritual director, and our conversations opened me to God's leading. Prior to this I had only spoken about my support of women's ordination privately. Now the inner journey I had been traveling all these years was about to become an outer one! Through this retreat experience, I came to see God was beckoning me to give voice publicly to the justice issue that all leadership and pastoral positions be open to women. I shared this experience, as well as the prayer I was inspired to write, with my spiritual director who had companioned me for the previous 19 years. I was shocked by his response, which was negative to the extreme. He told me, "It doesn't matter whether it's 20 years, 200 years, or 2,000 years from now, women will never be ordained, because it's God's will." I saw clearly that, in his eyes, it was okay for me to have differing opinions privately but not publicly—even if God was leading me to speak out. My growing freedom allowed me to leave this established direction relationship and seek a new one that would be open to God's Spirit, wherever that would lead.

Another result of that retreat was the birth of a faith-sharing group, which continues to meet 11 years later. Our first topic was "Jesus Challenges Society's Perception of Women"—a practical and prayerful way to give voice publicly to this issue. I came once again to a new way of being in relationship with the institutional church. God led me from a safe route to one that would stretch me. This new relationship challenged me to use more fully the gift of inner freedom I had received through mutual forgiveness in 1993. God's clear call was to listen carefully to the Spirit and to be open, humble, respectful, honest, and free as I publicly responded to injustices in the church. A few examples of these responses included the need to broaden restrictive language used to describe God in prayer and worship; to continue to include women in the Holy Thursday foot-washing ritual; and to lead a pastoral and parish action team response to the clergy sex-abuse scandal.

Trail to the Summit of Gray's Peak, Colorado
Elevation 14,270 feet

Further Growth in Education

In 2005 I entered the Spiritual Direction Program at Neumann University in Aston, Pennsylvania, and graduated in 2009 with a M. S. in Spiritual Direction. My experience in the program was pivotal to my faith journey in four important ways. It brought me more deeply into the contemplative part of the catholic tradition. The spiritual direction skills gave me additional ways to companion people in their faith journey. The contemplative stance of the professors and the classes, as well as the readings and the writing assignments, broadened my mind, deepened my heart, and transformed my being. And finally, with each course and each experience in this program, my heart became freer and more trusting as I walked on new spiritual ground.

During this program I took two courses in the History of Christian Spirituality where we studied the great Christian writers—Benedict, Julian of Norwich, Teresa of Avila, John of the Cross, Ignatius Loyola, and other contemplatives—whose spirit is at the heart of the catholic tradition as passed on to us through the centuries. Each student posed a question to be answered by the writings of these authors. As it turned out, these two questions and the answers I received were integral to my journey.

In the fall of 2005 my first question was: How can I be faithful to God's call to be broad, inclusive, and just while I am feeling the narrowness, restrictions, and injustice of the institutional church? In brief, I learned through the wisdom of these writers how to go beyond what the church edicts say, not be restricted by them, yet be rooted in and connected to its rich spirit as directed by Jesus. Surrender, humility, and love coupled with a questioning, free, and persevering spirit are the key elements of their wisdom that have sustained me on my journey of faithfulness to God's call.

Living into this question and the wisdom of the answers led me to worship occasionally with a local Protestant congregation, whose pastor was a woman. I needed at times to hear a woman preach, something that, because of church law, never happened in my parish. Beginning in late 2007, I also began worshipping occasionally with the St. Mary Magdalene Community, an intentional catholic community in Drexel Hill, Pennsylvania, pastored by Roman Catholic Womanpriest (RCWP) Eileen McCafferty DiFranco. I found it to be an inclusive and just community and its worship far more authentic. Around the time I began this course in 2005, the

Grand Jury report in Philadelphia was released, implicating many priests and bishops in the sex-abuse scandal and cover-up. As Pastoral Associate, I led an effort by members of our parish community to enter into dialogue with the archdiocesan leadership. Their flat refusal to meet with us stung, both emotionally and spiritually. In the face of injustice, horrendous crime, and the subsequent cover-up, they closed the door—and once again God called me to go beyond the closed door. We continued with several other actions in the parish to help our people work through their grief, pain, and distress.

Another experience underlying my question to these writers was in youth ministry. During Eucharistic celebrations, our high school teens and others were invited to come around the altar. The physical closeness enhanced their experience of God and one another, and they so enjoyed and appreciated this more intimate worship. Unfortunately, changes from Rome eliminated this. Here again I struggled: How do I implement a rule that I know from experience is not in the best interest of God's people? The Vatican also made rules restricting Eucharistic ministers from cleansing the communion vessels; only the ordained could now clean them. This narrow rule kept people in the community from something they had done for years and placed a divide between clergy and laity. Other liturgical changes also tightened the box I was working in. The last crisis for me, in 2009, which centered around a Holy Week foot-washing ritual, was a clarifying moment in my discernment. I knew I could no longer work in this ever-narrowing, claustrophobic box. I had to leave. I found a door—and ventured into the unknown.

Mount Abraham, Lincoln Gap, Vermont
After hiking to the summit of mountains, my husband and I
often place our feet on the marker located at its highest point.

In the fall of 2009, I began my second course in Christian Spirituality and posed this question to the writers: How can I be a healing, transforming presence in a wounded church that has wounded me deeply? The answer to this question had been unfolding. The spiritual writers spoke to me about freedom of heart, letting go of comfortable ministry, and radical willingness to search out and walk the path where God leads me. By the time I began this course, I had experienced two defining moments in 2009 that contributed to the formulation of this question. I had left my position on the parish pastoral staff in May (a fuller explanation is in the next section) and in July attended an Interfaith Spiritual Direction Conference. During this conference, I experienced a significant God-moment. The presenter from the Christian tradition led us through a contemplative reflection on the baptism of Jesus. During the sharing that followed, an attendee said that as a woman in the Catholic church she had an uneven relationship with Jesus. The presenter responded that the Catholic church's teaching of holding Jesus as high priest and then excluding women from the priesthood is a major issue and a source of deep pain for some women. During the presenter's genuine, honest, and loving response, I felt a crippling pain in my heart and literally felt my wounded heart and soul fall onto the floor. During this time I was acutely aware of God's presence and sorrow for my suffering. This intense "heart" experience continued to unfold as we then contemplated the Emmaus story, where the disciples left Jerusalem, that holy place where Jesus was crucified, and traveled to Emmaus. After all they had witnessed, their eyes had been opened to all Jesus had taught them, and they were transformed. After this they returned to Jerusalem as transformed disciples prepared to share the Good News. I, too, had recently left the church, a place of pain and suffering for me. Yet I knew that at some point, after being to my Emmaus, I would also return, be transformed in a new way, and be ready to share the Good News.

Ayers Track, Stowe, Vermont
This hike provided an unusually beautiful scene of brilliant leaves peeking out from the freshly fallen snow in October 2015.

Pain and Moving Forward

Prior to this summer conference, I had sensed that God was leading me into another place in ministry. In May 2009 after a 2 ½ year discernment process, I realized God was leading me to leave the staff of St. Francis Parish. So after 15 years on the pastoral staff and 14 years of volunteer ministry prior to that, I left St. Francis. Although staying was painful, my leaving was a difficult decision and hugely unsettling. It was so hard to leave because I loved the people of St. Francis—and still do. But God was calling and I knew I had to go. The great gift of inner freedom allowed me to leave and start a new chapter in my life. Freedom allowed me to begin a wilderness walk of deep trust.

As I began walking this path, I first needed to work through, at many different levels, leaving my lifelong church community, as well as the pain of experiences that violated my deep sense of call. This was indeed a time of much-needed healing. I felt wounded and needed to take time to reflect and heal. An unexpected and significant moment of healing occurred one warm, early summer day. I was taking a long walk, enjoying the gentle breeze and reflecting on my experiences. Several miles from home the heavens opened and rain gushed forth by the bucketful! As water drenched my entire being, I felt it cleansing my wounded heart. Water seeped into every pore and reached into my depths. Saturated from head to toe, I smiled, looked upward, and felt a lightening within. With each raindrop, I felt God's tangible, healing touch.

At this point I want to discuss more fully my feelings of woundedness, because addressing these was essential to both my healing and my deepening inner freedom. The woundedness was related to my ideas or presence being pushed aside, ignored, or rejected in pastoral situations over a number of years. I had many opportunities to minister pastorally and will always be grateful for these graced moments. There were, however, numerous other times when I was unable to minister as I felt called to do. Here are some examples.

- As a bereavement minister I felt called to lead burial services. I offered to do this and stood ready to do so whenever the need arose. However, my pastor never asked me to lead them. Only the deacons and priests were allowed to conduct them. Once when a bereavement team member had died, I asked our pastor if I could lead the service with him. He graciously agreed. It was a grace-filled time, and I hoped to be able to do this as needed in the future. I had tasted freedom and experienced what I now believed I was called to do. Although I was ready to do this whenever called upon and the pastor said he was open to it, the priests never again asked me to lead. I was emotionally distressed and frustrated being so close to freedom, which was again denied to me. When the pastor allowed a man studying to be a deacon to lead these services, it became clear to me that only the ordained men would do so. I knew this door was closed.
- Ministering to the sick as a non-ordained person was sometimes problematic. I could pray with them and offer them communion but could not anoint them. People in these dire situations often want the anointing as well. I was restricted from being able to minister as the situation required. It was frustrating for me to not have the freedom to fully assist people in their need.
- Another experience occurred when a member of the parish died suddenly. No priest was available. When a parishioner in an official capacity called, I offered to go to the scene and be with the family; but he said no, he would call the neighboring parish for a priest. I felt the sting and pain of his choosing someone outside our parish to

minister to the family solely in order to have an ordained priest present.

- Several times during my 15 years on the pastoral staff our parish hosted the Community Thanksgiving Service, an ecumenical service sponsored by the Springfield Ministerium. Many community churches participated in this wonderful, long-standing tradition. I enjoyed these grace-filled moments and was actively involved in preparing and coordinating the prayer service. However, I was not free to lead any part of the service because I was not ordained—and I was not ordained solely because I was a woman. Each time this happened, I felt the injustice, frustration, and pain of exclusion at not being able to answer the call within me to lead public prayer.

- The language and imagery describing God during our parish Eucharistic celebrations reflected only male imagery. God's self has been revealed to me more broadly and in many ways, such as Mother, Midwife, Womb of Creation, Heart of Love, Forever Friend. I had outlined a process of education and gradual introduction into the parish liturgies of additional images and broader language to describe the Divine, God, the Indescribable. This would have been an educational experience included in the parish religious education program and the parish school curriculum. It also would have been a pastoral one, as part of our Sunday worship, other liturgies, and prayer experiences. We already were using this broader language during many of our parish staff prayer gatherings. This suggestion, however, was ignored and pushed aside, even after following up with the pastor. It became clear that this door was closed, freedom denied. I felt once again the deep pain of being shut off. I felt the striking paradox of being told that I, as a woman, was made in God's image; yet we never used a feminine image of God during the prayers of our Eucharistic liturgies. This was hurtful at the deepest level because it struck at the very core of my being.

These were all important, albeit painful, experiences of exclusion on my journey into freedom. In each case I could only go so far. I could not anoint or lead burials because I wasn't ordained. I wasn't ordained because I was a woman. In each situation I was excluded and my freedom to answer God's call denied. I came to realize that, in order to minister fully, I had to be ordained.

This pain, however, has yielded several gifts for which I am grateful—awareness, a clear vision of discrimination, freedom, new life, and a deeper appreciation for the suffering that victims of injustice and discrimination feel. I would not be the person I am today without having traveled the road of struggle and pain on the pathway to freedom. Pain—feeling it, experiencing it fully, and doing the hard work of journeying through it—was an essential part of the transforming fire that led me to freedom.

During this time of needed healing in 2009, I also prayed while contemplating Joyce Rupp's book *Open the Door—A Journey to the True Self*, which helped me be in touch with my feelings and the path God was calling me to walk. The prayers, writings, and reflections offered in this book opened within me inner doorways to freedom. They invited me to experience my feelings of woundedness, embrace them, and be transformed by them. Over several months, these heart-opening moments of prayerful reflection helped me move into the freedom I craved.

Jonkershoek Nature Reserve, Stellenbosch, South Africa

Awakening to the Call for Courage

In July 2009, I experienced a truly significant moment during a spiritual direction session with my director, whom I had begun seeing in 2006. After I had shared a recent experience of leading worship and giving a homily, my director posed a simple, four-word question: "What does this mean?" Without hesitation I said, "It means I have to fully explore the possibility of ordination." With these words I felt a monumental awakening well up within me. Because of the Catholic church's rules, ordination had not even been a blip on my radar screen. Now God was insisting I search out this path. I was profoundly shaken. What I previously thought was a justice issue for women, I now realized was also a deeply personal call for me.

I had asked my director if she would anoint me during our session. When she asked how I wanted to be anointed, I told her to anoint me however the Spirit moved her and to pray whatever words were on her heart. It was an explosive experience of God I will never forget. I expected her to pray for my healing. Yet as she generously anointed my forehead, eyes, ears, mouth, hands, and feet with oil, she prayed for openness to God's call and courage to walk whatever path lay before me. My sensory experience of God was extraordinary, and I felt within myself a deep freedom of heart and mind. I expected healing and found that healing in awakening to the possibility of following a path into priesthood—the call of my heart.

These were important and memorable moments on my journey into freedom!

An awe-inspiring sunrise hike in the Outback, Australia

Vision of Freedom

In May 2009, I had begun worshipping with the St. Mary Magdalene (SMM) Community every week. The SMM Community is like the early Christian communities. When the leader isn't there, someone else steps in to lead. So in late June/early July 2009 I had the opportunity to lead worship and to give a homily. After giving the homily, I remember telling my husband, "You know, I've listened to a lot of homilies. Some have been really good and others not so good, but this was the first time I was *allowed* to give a homily." Something inside me was calling out to be expressed, and I knew that I needed to do this on a regular basis—not just a few times a year. In that moment I knew I could no longer allow an unjust church law to keep me from being who I am. I knew in my heart I had to explore the call to ordination. I could no longer push this call aside; I needed to place it front and center and discern whether God was calling me to ordination. When I sat with that thought, I felt rocked to the core.

      Here I was 55 years old seriously contemplating ordained ministry—God was shaking my foundation like an 8.0 earthquake or gigantic tsunami. And so the adventure hike I had been on with God all these years suddenly became wildly adventurous! I had no desire to leave the Catholic church. I loved the rich contemplative and liturgical rituals and celebrations of Catholicism that became part of who I am. This was home to me. So many have asked me why I didn't leave the Catholic church and join a church that recognized women's ordination. It is a mystery to me, because based on logic alone I would have left. But something more, something deeper than logic— the spiritual call of my heart—was leading me to stay and walk another path in the catholic tradition. I therefore pursued ordination in the Roman Catholic Womenpriests Community.[2] Roman Catholic Womenpriests provided a path for me to answer this call and be ordained in apostolic succession. I am very grateful to the women who began this movement and on whose shoulders I stand, and to those with whom I journey today. It is important to remember the embryonic beginnings of my call to priesthood date back to 1985. After a time of contemplative prayer I remember at the depth of my being saying "if the Catholic church ordained married women, I would be a priest." I never articulated that to anyone until July 2009 when I knew I had to fully explore the call to ordination.

*At the summit, Stan and Caryl
Connemara National Park, Ireland*

Freedom Found

In December 2009, shortly after I was accepted as a candidate for ordination in the Roman Catholic Womenpriests Community, I articulated the defining moment before me: Am I willing to listen to the Spirit of God and do what God asks no matter what the cost or will I follow a man-made church rule and say no to the Spirit of God? I freely answered yes to God's call. It was a Gethsemane[3] moment of soul-searching that required every ounce of freedom's desire and courage within me. I made this decision out of love—love for God, love for the People of God, and love for myself.

Canon 1024 in the law of the Roman Catholic Church states that "Only a baptized man (vir) validly receives sacred ordination." When I chose to walk the path into ordination, the call of my heart, it was not with the intention of breaking a church law. I walked this path because of the deep, soul-stimulating sense of call. Breaking the church law was merely the result of answering the call from God and the community. This has resulted in excommunication. Because of my ordination, officially I have been excommunicated from the Roman Catholic church. Yet I do not feel excommunicated. The people of God—*who are the church*—have called me to priesthood. I feel closer to God than ever before because I have listened and followed God's call deep within me and expressed through God's people.

Throughout the time of preparation for ordination and continuing discernment of this call, I was faithfully companioned by many people—my husband, our three children, my spiritual director, faith-sharing friends, other womenpriests, the St. Mary Magdalene Community, and close friends. I could not have answered this call without them, and I continue to be grateful for their strong, loving support.

As I walked this prophetic path trusting in the Spirit of God and discerning the voices of community, I felt freer than I ever had. I was ordained a deacon in May 2010. During the time I was an ordained deacon, I was able for the first time to publicly respond to the injustice of prohibiting the ordination of women. The Vatican had issued a document stating that the ordination of women and pedophilia were grave offenses. I wrote a letter in response, which was published in the July 23, 2010 issue of *The Philadelphia Inquirer.* I believe this letter (below) reflected my growing inner freedom.

> "As an ordained deacon in the Roman Catholic Womenpriests Community, I would like to respond to the article 'Vatican revises sex-abuse laws' (last Friday).
>
> Pedophilia and the ordination of women were stated as grave offenses in a recent Vatican document. Linking these in the same document is misleading to society and misrepresents the intent of the women's ordination movement. Pedophilia is a criminal act in violation of the moral law of humanity. The ordination of women is an act of prophetic obedience to the spirit of God and is in response to a call from God and the community. It is in violation of an unjust, man-made church law.
>
> Pedophilia gravely harms children; women's gifts in ordained ministry serve the community.
>
> The distinction is clear."

Ordination—At Last!

In June 2011, with over 300 people in attendance, I, a married woman, was ordained a Catholic priest. The joy was overwhelming! Although this was only a moment along the path, it was an incredibly deep experience that I will forever remember. My husband and three children, along with other family and friends, enthusiastically took part in the ordination ceremony. During the singing of the Litany of Saints, as I lay prostrate—surrendered completely to God—I felt the Spirit's powerful, palpable presence throughout the entire gathering. We felt heaven and earth unite, and there was a tangible experience of oneness in that moment. During this prayer I saw the faces of holy men and women in my life—both living and deceased—as they were present to me. I also felt God's presence in a powerful way as I was ordained through the laying on of hands. My friend, Mary LeFever, whom I mentioned earlier in my story as the one who hoped to live long enough to see me become a priest, was one of the people who laid hands on me. In 2009 she told me why I should be a priest. "It's your presence, the way you proclaim scripture and minister eucharist, your compassion, how you lead prayer, how you minister to those grieving. You reflect God, and we feel God through you." Through the laying on of hands her words came full circle, and I publicly accepted the call to priesthood. This joyful ordination experience was an extraordinary celebration that marked a significant milestone on my journey into freedom. This path into priesthood has truly been the most freeing and surprising walk I have ever taken. My hiking boots will never be the same! I finally could be who I am. I have always loved adventure, hiking new trails, and traveling to new places. In fact, my husband and I and our children have hiked up many challenging mountains and along many beautiful trails over the last 35 years. This adventure of the spirit, into priesthood, is yet another hike into the wilderness, full of challenge and beauty. I believe God is using my adventurous streak to help create a new path in the catholic tradition, however that path unfolds.

Caryl at her Priestly Ordination in 2011

Tyler Arboretum, Media, Pennsylvania

    The following poem, which I wrote during my final ordination preparations early in 2011, captures the essence of my journey into freedom.

The Call

Love—free and plentiful from my wonderful
parents—
    showed me God's heart.
Into adulthood I was there
    pushing the edges, standing for justice
    in the workplace and in faith life—
    leading others, bringing people together.
Walking the path of faith
    I struggled.
Injustice toward women in the church seared
my heart
    yet God called me to stay—
    and I knew deep inside
    my call was to reform the church from within.
Staying—answering the call—was both struggle and joy—
    a mystery indeed.
    Logic said leave yet my heart—beyond
    doubt—said stay.
Learning—following my heart—ministering to people in
their deepest needs—
    I found God ever present.
Giving voice to the God within me meant speaking for
justice
    with love, truth, and humility.
The justice issue of women's leadership in the church
    burned in my heart.
The call became so strong—the church restrictions
became so tight—
    I searched for a way to stay, minister, and work for
    justice.

Authenticity prevailed.
    I left the familiar and walked on new
    ground.
Letting go—I risked—and hiked into the wilderness
    not knowing where the path would
    lead.
Companions were many. mature in God's ways. open to the Spirit.
    They walked with me—called me to
    ordination—
    family, friends, spiritual companions,
    colleagues, contemporary authors,
    spiritual giants in tradition.
To answer my call their companionship is a necessity and pure gift.
With inner freedom—I explored
    ordination and finally embraced fully
    God's call—the community's call.
Trusting mightily I walk the path
    and find a prophetic call rising within
    me.
The call to leadership. The call to radical, inclusive love. The call to priesthood.
    I answer Yes.

Tyler Arboretum, Media, Pennsylvania
The sunshine and shadows on this lush summer trail reflect life's wonders and realities.

Living Joyfully With Freedom

Walking into ordained ministry—priesthood—has opened doors and brought me onto paths in ways I never would have expected.

One of these paths has been in officiating weddings. I have listened to the painful experiences of those whose religious institutions were unwilling to witness their marriage. Now having the freedom to witness and celebrate the union of so many people of different faith traditions has been a great source of joy for me. In one case I officiated the marriage of a Jewish woman and a Muslim man. The unity felt through their marriage and among the diverse guests was profound—truly a gift from God! Another wonderful moment—I had the extraordinary experience of officiating my daughter's and son-in-law's wedding. What a joy and privilege it was to witness their marriage! Other moments have included baptisms in many different venues, funeral and burial services, and anointings of the sick, both in community and individual settings. The spiritual and emotional intimacy of these moments is deeply moving, and I am grateful for the freedom to minister fully to God's people in their deepest joys and needs. Additional joy and freedom moments include leading and celebrating ecumenical eucharists and prayer services with other church communities and participation in the Upper Darby Ministerium, which has opened doors of outreach to the community and strengthened relationships between community organizations.

 Sharing my story with university students (religion classes at Penn State Abington), with women's groups, and with community groups both in the United States and South Africa has led me into greater freedom. Each time I tell my story something more is transformed within me. Their questions reach into my soul, and when I respond I find deeper healing and freedom. For these unexpected gifts, I am so grateful.

 I have also had the privilege of companioning other women in RCWP as they prepare for ordination. The spiritual and emotional intimacy of this relationship is extraordinary. For me, witnessing their first steps into the call they have had for years and are finally free to answer has been pure gift. In 2014 I had the opportunity to travel to South Africa for the ordination of the second South African womanpriest. What a thrill it was to be in South Africa and experience the beauty and joy of these people. Experiencing this beautiful country and witnessing the ordination of my friend has been a highlight of my life. This experience not only brought me into close relationship with the woman who was ordained, but also with her family, her community, and her country in ways I had never thought possible. I marvel at how the Spirit of God has interwoven our lives. In 2016 I had the privilege of returning for the priestly ordination of the third South African woman. It was a delightful and graced time to reconnect with people I had met previously and to establish new relationships. Companioning others into priesthood in the United States and in other countries has been an unexpected and wonderful part of my journey into freedom.

    Co-pastoring the St. Mary Magdalene (SMM) Community, who has called me to priesthood, has been foundational to my ministry. Serving her members and journeying with them into deeper relationship with God and one another provides the nourishment and challenge to grow and move wherever the Spirit of God leads. I am so happy in the SMM Community, and I love the people dearly. They continue to teach me more about life, inclusive love, and generous service. The freedom to create, nurture, and empower inclusive communities open to the leading of God's Spirit is a special gift I have received through this call.

For as long as I can remember I have had an interfaith heart, and it pained me when people were excluded from receiving communion. A personal example is my husband Stan, who is Presbyterian. He had worshipped regularly with our family at St. Francis of Assisi Church but could not receive communion. I knew how deeply spiritual he was, and it saddened me that he was excluded from the table. Now it is a great joy for me to witness him receiving communion as part of our St. Mary Magdalene Community. I feel blessed and delighted to now be free to invite people of any faith tradition to partake of our inclusive communion table. I have found great joy and freedom in being a member of an inclusive community where all are truly welcome and where we freely share many inspirational, interspiritual writings during our Sunday worship.

I also experienced freedom in an unexpected place. In April 2015 my dear 93-year-old stepmother, Rose, died. She wanted to be buried from her beloved St. Francis of Assisi Parish, where I had served as Pastoral Associate for 15 years. At first I felt unsettled going back to the rectory to plan her funeral Mass because I would again be limited in what I could do. I was going back to St. Francis Parish as an ordained Catholic priest, but would be restricted because the institutional church does not recognize my ordination. Yet there was something different in this experience. As in the Emmaus story, I came back healed, transformed, and ready to share the Good News in my being. I was able to draw from the radical, inclusive love at the heart of my call to priesthood and return there freely choosing to love, no matter what happened or what anyone would say. I am so grateful, for the people were kind and compassionate and the experience was freeing. Truly a graced moment. As the priest leading the funeral Mass incensed Rose's body toward the end of the liturgy, I too incensed her body in the only way I was allowed. As we sang the *Song of Farewell*, I incensed her with my voice. This entire occasion at the parish where I had experienced both great joy and deep pain was a Good News moment, fueled by forgiveness, that brought me more deeply into freedom.

In 1983, when I came so close to leaving the church, I never would have predicted the incredible, life-giving journey that has unfolded. I have written my story, not in protest, but in gratitude. The pain and messiness of my journey has been a transforming fire that led me to follow a very personal, life-changing call. The freedom to experience God in people and ways that had been beyond my reach prior to ordination is a gift I greatly cherish and is an ever-unfolding journey.

A Story for Everyone...

I think if I could put what I learned from this journey into a few sentences it would be this: We need to be free to be who we are. We are all called to be in different places—business, education, healthcare, politics, ministry, counseling, or wherever our hearts want to go. We need to find out what that call is, and then pursue it and be it.

My prayer is that every person will experience the warmth of God's loving embrace. My dream is that everyone will strive to be their authentic selves. My hope is that someday we will all journey freely into who we really are.

Reading, Pennsylvania
Birds flying freely...

Footnotes

[1]Ignatius of Loyola was a 16th century writer, whose spirituality considered all experiences as gift. He believed God could use both good and difficult times for good purposes.

[2]Roman Catholic Womenpriests (RCWP) is a movement that began in Europe in 2002 and moved to North America in 2005. Those in RCWP are ordained in apostolic succession. Male bishops in good standing with Rome were involved in the first ordinations, and the women bishops, ordained in apostolic succession, have continued in this tradition. For further information on the history of RCWP please see their website www.romancatholicwomenpriests.org.

[3]The Garden of Gethsemane was the place Jesus experienced a time of soul-searching and struggle just prior to his passion.

An Interview with the Author

To hear more of Caryl's story, an interview with her can be seen at https://bit.ly/carylconroyjohnson

Acknowledgments

I am grateful to the many people who have companioned me on my journey into freedom. This story could not have been written without them. I owe special thanks to the following people:

To my dear husband, Stan—Thank you for your honest and loving suggestions that gave fuller expression to my story. I am forever grateful for you.

To our wonderful children, Dayna, Tahra, and Shaen—Thanks for reading my story. Your suggestions and comments brought it life!

To Janet Badolato, my good friend and neighbor—Thank you for your careful reading and wonderful suggestions. You helped me express my thoughts, feelings, and life experiences with greater freedom.

To Anne Hayden, my friend and faith-sharing companion—Many thanks for listening to my "story behind the words" and for your thought-provoking suggestions. You made it better.

To Fran Cuneo, my long-time friend and spiritual partner—For your faithful companionship and feedback and for interviewing me with joy and genuineness, I am deeply grateful.

To Maria Marlowe, my friend and fellow journeyer in faith—Thank you for reading my story, for your suggestions, and for your professional editing. You gave it the finish it needed!

To Mary Ryan, my kindred-spirit friend and sister priest in South Africa—Thank you for the writing tips and framework that got me started and the suggestions that moved me forward. I will always be grateful for your encouragement, support, and loving presence across the miles.

To Kathleen Gibbons Schuck, my friend and sister priest—My deepest thanks for your technical support for the interview and for producing the video. Your upbeat manner and clear instructions gave us the focus we needed.